Heart to Heart

CONNECTING WITH YOUR CHILD

Jeff Goelitz & Elyse April

Illustrations by Laura Stagno

The Family & World Health Series

HOHM PRESS
Chino Valley, Arizona

Cover Design, Interior Design and Layout: Zachary Parker, Kadak Graphics
Illustrations: Laura Stagno, www.laurastagno.com

Library of Congress Cataloging-in-Publication Data

Goelitz, Jeff.
Heart to heart : connecting with your child / Jeff Goelitz & Elyse April ;
illustrations by Laura Stagno.
   pages cm. -- (The family & world health series)
ISBN 978-1-935387-43-5 (trade pbk. : alk. paper)
1. Parent and child. 2. Parenting. 3. Communication in families. I.
April, Elyse. II. Title.
HQ755.85.G64 2013
306.874--dc23
                    2013004591

Hohm Press
P.O. Box 4410
Chino Valley, AZ 86323
800-381-2700
http://www.hohmpress.com

This book was printed in China.

Dedication

For parents and caregivers whose love and role-modeling shapes
the hearts and minds of children.

Acknowledgements

Special thanks to Laura Stagno, our brilliant illustrator, whose sensitive and playful characters have so beautifully reflected the essence of positive, heart-based adult-child communications. Further congratulations to the whole Stagno family, as Laura's first child was birthed in synchronicity to the release of this book.

Much appreciation to Doc Childre, founder of HeartMath, whose inspirational ideas and practical techniques have influenced many, many people.

There is a different kind of listening that helps parents and caregivers communicate with children—listening to the wisdom of our hearts.

When we listen to our hearts, we are better able to connect with our children and ourselves.

Parents often feel overwhelmed from working—at their jobs, or at home cleaning and shopping—to support their family's needs.

To help strengthen the connection with children, take a few minutes from your busy day to be fully present with your child. Slow down and take a few deep breaths. Kneel down so you can look into your child's eyes and softly ask, "How are you? What are you doing? Can I help?"

When children are upset or frustrated, ask questions to help them solve their own problems. "What things can we do to solve this problem? What can we do to help?"

Inviting children to try solving their own problems helps build their confidence, creativity, and intelligence.

When your child is having a hard time, listening may be all that is needed to help the child feel calmer and supported.

Listening is not fixing a problem. Listening is a way of bringing two hearts together— one can be struggling and the other can be understanding and compassionate.

Children learn by example. When we show children how we care for ourselves or others when feeling stress, they learn how to better deal with disappointment and change.

The best way to care for ourselves or others is to pause and listen to our hearts. What does my heart say? What attitude or action can help us deal with the problem?

Sometimes children get scared by imaginary things. We may not see, feel or hear what they do, but our children still need our comfort and understanding.

Be smart when praising your child. Don't overpraise. The right kind of praise builds your child's inner confidence.

Praise your child for his or her effort and hard work. Praise what you see.

"You worked really hard on that puzzle. You must feel proud of yourself," instead of, "I'm so proud of you."

"I appreciate how you helped clean the table," instead of, "You are such a good girl."

When you need to discipline children, they will hear you better when you speak from your heart rather than react with anger or frustration. The feeling behind what you say is as important as what you say.

The "Shift and Shine" technique (described in the notes in the back) can help family members listen more deeply when someone is upset. This is a simple way to invite a child or adult back into a heartfelt relationship.

Having a heart-to-heart talk about what you appreciate is a special activity to do during the day or at bedtime.
Sharing something that you are grateful for, even if it was a hard day, helps build stronger hearts and minds together.

Play brings joy to our lives! Sing, play games, laugh, read or tell stories together. Play keeps our hearts flexible and strong.

When hearts are full, joy can surprise us at any moment. Practice these habits daily to help your family become closer and create more love together.

It is just a heartbeat away!

HELPFUL INFORMATION FOR THE PARENT AND CAREGIVER

Appreciation

Appreciation means to be sincerely thankful or grateful for someone or something. To add more appreciation to your parent-child relationship, write up a list of 4-5 qualities that you appreciate about your child. Post the list on a wall so you can review it daily. Appreciate your child's actions when he or she does something well that is out of the ordinary: "Thank you for helping by picking up your things," or "When you laugh, it makes me smile." Be honest and descriptive in your appreciation, not phony. At bedtime, take turns sharing with your child some of the things you appreciated during the day.

The Shift and Shine Technique®

To strengthen your own and your child's experience of appreciation, practice the Shift and Shine Technique together.

Using the Technique for the First time

Parent asks child: ***Who or what do we care about?***

First model an answer by telling your child who *you* care about. Then ask your child who *they* care about?

Ask: ***When you love or care for someone or something, where do you feel that love?*** Put your hand over your heart (center of the chest, as a visible clue).

Parent asks: ***What is shift? ….. (child answers if he or she has an answer)***

Then Parent can go on to say: ***Shift means to move or change, such as going from sad to happy or moving from one place to another.*** Demonstrate the meaning of shift by shifting from one position to another.

Parent asks: ***Do you ever have a warm feeling in your heart when you feel love or care for someone? It's kind of like the warmth from the sun.*** [Give child time to answer before continuing.] ***Have you ever felt the warmth of the sun on your skin?*** [Give child time to answer.] ***What does that feel like?*** [Give child time to answer.] ***When we feel love, appreciation or care for someone, it's like the warmth from the sun shining in our hearts.***

Step 1:
Parent suggests to child: *Begin by putting your attention on the area around your heart or the center of your chest.*

Parent: Model by putting your hand over your heart.

Step 2:
Parent instructs child: *Now pretend to breathe in and out of your heart area. Take three slow breaths.*

Parent: Model the breathing.

Step 3:
Parent explains: *Think of someone or something that makes you feel happy, like your Mom or Dad or maybe a special place that you visit, like a park. Feel that happy feeling in your heart and then shine that feeling to someone or something special.*

Parent: Let your child experience the feeling for a few seconds. The length of time will increase with each experience. Bedtime is one of the best times to practice Shift and Shine.

Making Shift and Shine a New Habit (optional depending on space)
To make this technique a new habit, practice Steps 1, 2 and 3 several times a day. In the beginning, it is easier to learn the Shift and Shine technique when you are feeling calm and not stressed-out about something.

Here are some times during the day when you might practice Shift and Shine for 2-3 minutes.
Which ones will work for you?

- At the start of the day
- After lunch
- Before going to sleep
- Driving in the car
- In between events
- Taking a mid-morning break
- Waiting in line
- Before a stressful event or situation

For more helpful information, go to www.heartmath.org

OTHER TITLES OF INTEREST FROM HOHM PRESS

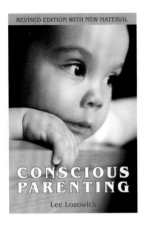

CONSCIOUS PARENTING
Revised Edition with New Material
by Lee Lozowick

Any individual who cares for children needs to attend to the essential message of this book: that the first two years are the most crucial time in a child's education and development, and that children learn to be healthy and "whole" by living with healthy, whole adults.

Hohm Press, Paper, $19.95, 336 pages.
ISBN: 978-1-935387-17-9

TO TOUCH IS TO LIVE
The Need for Genuine Affection in an Impersonal World

By Mariana Caplan
Foreword by Ashley Montagu

Offers positive solutions for countering the effects of the growing depersonalization of our times. "An important book that brings to the forefront the fundamentals of a healthy world.' – Patch Adams, M.D.

Hohm Press, Paper, 272 pages, $19.95
ISBN: 978-1-890772-24-6

PARENTING, A SACRED TASK
10 Basics of Conscious Childraising
by Karuna Fedorschak

Highlights 10 basic elements that every parent can use to meet the everyday demands of childraising. "Thank you to Karuna Fedorschak for reminding us that parenting is a sacred task." – Peggy O'Mara, Editor and Publisher, *Mothering Magazine*.

Hohm Press, Paper, 158 pages, $12.95
ISBN: 978-1-890772-30-7

8 STRATEGIES FOR SUCCESSFUL STEP-PARENTING
by Nadir Baksh, Psy. D. and Laurie Elizabeth Murphy, R.N., Ph.D.

Becoming a step-parent, and "blending of families," is difficult work. The book presents 8 strategies, in the form of action steps, to maximize anyone's chances of success in this endeavor.

Hohm Press, Paper, 188 pages, $14.95
ISBN: 978-1-935387-08-4

To Order: 800-381-2700, or visit our website, www.hohmpress.com

OTHER TITLES OF INTEREST IN FAMILY & WORLD HEALTH SERIES

WE LIKE TO READ

A Picture Book for Pre-Readers & Parents

by Elyse April

Illustrations by Angie Thompson

Provides a new look at how to teach and encourage reading by using play and "attachment parenting" — i.e., lots of physical closeness and learning by example. The upbeat rhyming format provides cues for parents and caregivers on how to provide a foundation for reading while enticing children with game-like activities.

Kalindi Press, Paper; 32 pages; $9.95; (English) ISBN: 978-1-890772-80-2; (Bi-Lingual) ISBN: 978-1-890772-81-9

WE LIKE TO HELP COOK

by Marcus Allsop

Illustrations by Diane Iverson

All the young children in these brightly-colored picture are helping adults to prepare simple, healthy and delicious foods. Easy text, plus some rhymes, make the books easy to read, and appealing to both kids and parents. Children help themselves or assist the adults by performing many age-related tasks, like pouring, shaking, washing, mashing and mixing — actions that most young children love to do.

Kalindi Press, Paper; 32 pages; $9.95; (English) ISBN: 978-1-935826-05-7; (Bi-lingual) ISBN: 978-1-935826-00-2

WE LIKE TO EAT WELL

by Elyse April

Illustrations by Lewis Agrell

What we eat is vitally important for good health … and so is how we eat … where and when we eat … and how much we eat … This book encourages young children and parents to develop the healthy eating habits that can last for a lifetime.

Kalindi Press, Paper; 32 pages; $9.95; (English) ISBN: 978-1-890772-69-7; (Bi-Lingual) ISBN: 978-1-935826-01-9

WE LIKE TO LIVE GREEN

by Mary Young

Design by Zachary Parker

This Earth-friendly book introduces to vital environmental themes in ways that will appeal to both young children and adults. We can all recycle and reuse, conserve water or grow a garden! Lively full-color photo montages demonstrate how to make a difference.

Kalindi Press, Paper, 32 pages, $9.95; (English) ISBN: 978-1-935387-00-8; (Bi-Lingual) ISBN: 978-1-935387-01-5

To Order: 800-381-2700, or visit our websites, www.kalindipress.com and www.familyhealthseries.com

ABOUT THE AUTHORS

Jeff Goelitz is currently a program developer, senior trainer and education specialist with the nonprofit Institute of HeartMath. He regularly consults with school professionals around the US to help improve classroom climate and performance. Jeff has authored *The College De-Stress Handbook*, and developed many programs to improve social and emotional learning.

Elyse April, MS (in Early Childhood Education, SUNY, New Paltz) since 2001 has devoted herself to advocacy for children, by writing, lecturing, and promoting books related to health and wellbeing for children and parents. She is the author of four titles in the Hohm Press/Kalindi Press *Family and World Health Series*.

VISIT OUR WEBSITES

www.hohmpress.com, www.kalindipress.com and www.familyhealthseries.com